The Complete Keyboard Player

BOOK 1

SONGS

To access companion recorded audio online, visit:
www.halleonard.com/mylibrary

Enter Code
6752-0685-6447-8033

ISBN: 978-0-7119-8356-4

EXCLUSIVELY DISTRIBUTED BY

HAL•LEONARD®

Published by
Wise Publications

T0052570

Contact us:
Hal Leonard
7777 West Bluemound Road
Milwaukee, WI 53213
Email: info@halleonard.com

In Europe, contact:
Hal Leonard Europe Limited
42 Wigmore Street
Marylebone, London, W1U 2RN
Email: info@halleonardeurope.com

In Australia, contact:
Hal Leonard Australia Pty. Ltd.
4 Lentara Court
Cheltenham, Victoria, 3192 Australia
Email: info@halleonard.com.au

Written and arranged by Kenneth Baker.
Music processed by Paul Ewers.
Edited by Sorcha Armstrong.

Cover & book design by Chloë Alexander Design.
Artist photographs courtesy of London Features International/ Redferns.

Audio recorded, mixed and mastered by Paul Honey.

Printed in the United Kingdom.

Your Guarantee of Quality
As publishers, we strive to produce every book to the highest commercial standards. This book has been carefully designed to minimise awkward page turns and to make playing from it a real pleasure.
Particular care has been given to specifying acid-free, neutral-sized paper made from pulps which have not been elemental chlorine bleached. This pulp is from farmed sustainable forests and was produced with special regard for the environment.
Throughout, the printing and binding have been planned to ensure a sturdy, attractive publication which should give years of enjoyment. If your copy fails to meet our high standards, please inform us and we will gladly replace it.

www.musicsales.com

About This Book

WELCOME TO THE fascinating world of home music-making.
This course will help you get the best out of your electronic keyboard – the most versatile instrument yet invented.

By the end of Book 1 you will be:

- **Reading Music**
- **Playing popular melodies** in many different styles
- **Easily adding complete accompaniments** consisting of bass notes, chords and drums to all your songs.

Although written primarily as a 'teach yourself' method, *The Complete Keyboard Player* books have been taken up eagerly by teachers (individual and classroom) all over the world.

This latest edition has been brought completely up to date, reflecting the changes and improvements in keyboards over the years, and introducing some new hit songs, while retaining many of the old favourites.

If you are teaching yourself to play, two helpful features have been retained from the earlier edition: the stickers – which remind you of the names of the notes, and the optional audio, in which you can hear how all the songs should sound, complete with a full band backing.

Good luck!

Kenneth Baker

Your Keyboard

ALTHOUGH MODERN KEYBOARDS vary from make to make and model to model, they all have the same basic features:

RHYTHM PATTERNS   INFORMATION SCREEN   SOLO SOUNDS

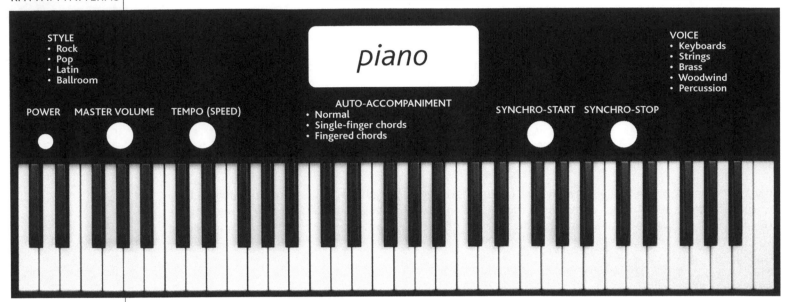

Power (mains)
Turns the keyboard on or off. Most keyboards can run on batteries or from the mains, using a suitable transformer, which is usually supplied with your keyboard.

Master Volume
This controls the overall 'loudness' of the instrument. It is either in the form of a slider, button or knob, which can be set anywhere from minimum to maximum.

Auto-accompaniment
This feature adds an automatic accompaniment to your melody, which you can use in various different ways.

Tempo (Speed)
This controls the speed of the accompaniment rhythm. Can be set anywhere from minimum to maximum, or may display an exact tempo, e.g. ♩=112. The number displayed is the number of beats per minute, and varies between about 45 to about 220.

Synchro-start
This button activates the auto-accompaniment and synchronises it to when you start playing.

Rhythm or Style
This feature adds a drum rhythm to your melody. You can choose between a number of different styles, e.g. rock, pop, latin, swing etc.

Voices or Solo Sounds
These might be grouped in different 'types' of voice, e.g. strings, woodwind, or they may be grouped by instrument, depending on how many different voices your particular keyboard offers. They add colour and interest to your melodies.

Information Screen
Most modern keyboards incorporate a digital screen which provides information about which settings you are using, e.g: which voice and rhythm you have selected, and whether you are using auto-accompaniment.

See your owner's manual for specific details.

Sitting At Your Keyboard

SET UP YOUR keyboard on its own stand or on a table of medium height.

Sit facing the centre of the instrument and adjust your seat so that your arms are level with the keyboard, or sloping down slightly towards it.

Support your hands from the wrists. Imagine that you are holding a rather fragile ball and curve your fingers lightly around it.

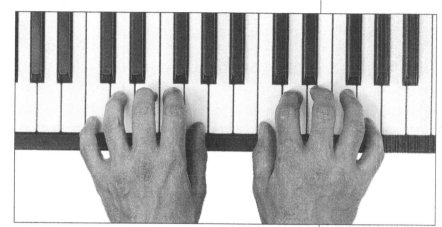

With the tips of your fingers, cover any five adjacent white notes in each hand.

This is your normal, most relaxed playing position. After all fingering and hand changes during a piece, you should return to this position.

Finger Numbers

Your fingers are numbered OUTWARDS from the thumbs, like this:

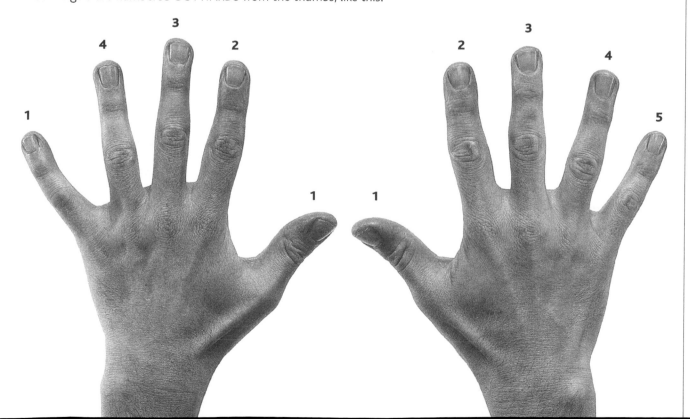

Warm Up

SWITCH ON YOUR KEYBOARD and turn up the **master volume**, and any subsidiary volume controls you may have, to about halfway.

Check that your **auto-accompaniment** control is switched to normal (or off):

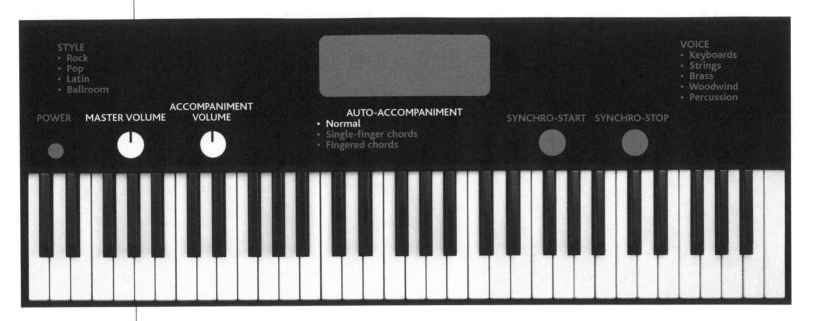

Select a voice, say **piano**:

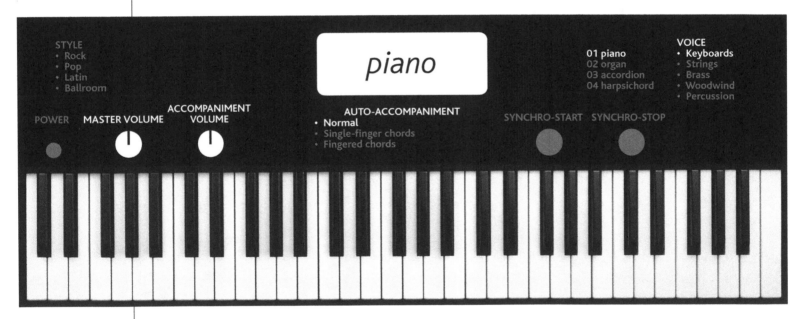

The **voices** (solo sounds) on your keyboard might be divided into general categories, such as **keyboards**, **woodwind**, **brass**, **strings**, and so on (a bit like an orchestra). In the example above, where we are aiming to set up a **piano**, go into **keyboards**, press **01** on the number pad (01 is an almost universal number set up for basic piano sound) and the piano sound will appear on the screen.

Run your finger along the keys from left to right and note the piano sounds progressing from Low to High. Now run your finger along the keys in the opposite direction and note the progression from High to Low.

Set up a **violin** sound for yourself. Go to **voices**, then **strings**. Find the number for violin and select it.
Play a few single notes at random in the middle to upper range of your keyboard and listen to the sound of the violin.

Now Let's Play Some Rhythm

THERE WILL BE MANY different rhythm patterns (sometimes called **styles**) available on your keyboard. Like voices, rhythms will probably be subdivided into **categories**. Typical rhythm categories are **rock**, **pop**, **ballroom** and **latin**:

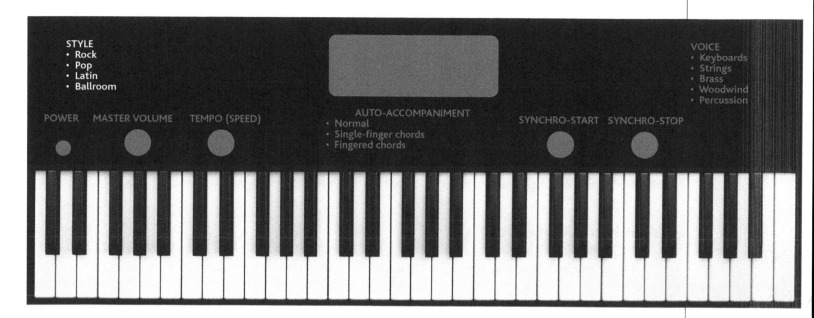

In your **rock** category, select one of the rock variations, for example **rock pop** and press **start**. Listen to this rhythm pattern for a few moments, then try speeding it up or slowing it down using your **tempo** control:

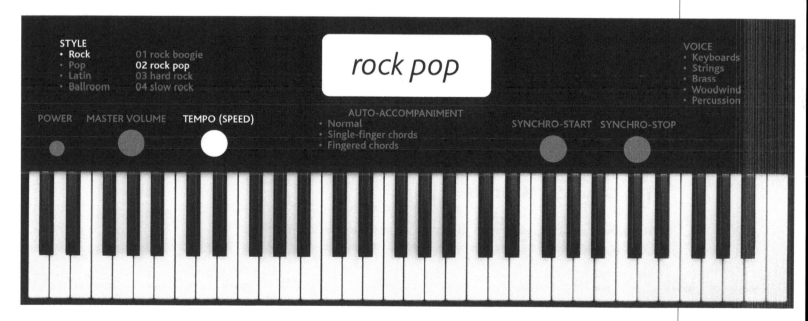

Try other rock variations, or totally different rhythms, such as **quickstep** (probably in the **ballroom** category) or **bossa nova** (probably in the **latin** category).

Now, instead of the **start** button, select **synchro**, or **synchro-start**.
Play any note in the lower register (the lower half of the keyboard) and the rhythm section will start automatically. Press **synchro** again and the rhythm will stop.

We shall be using this useful feature in a song soon.

Black And White Notes

YOUR KEYBOARD HAS a number of black and white keys*. The black keys are divided into groups of twos and threes, and these same groups repeat all along the keyboard:

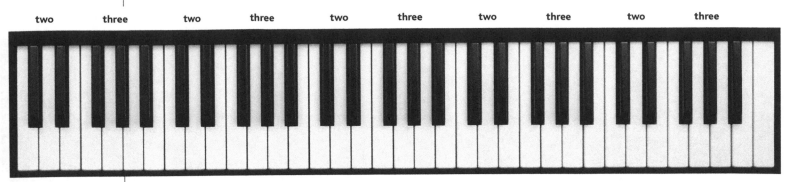

You need these black key groups in order to locate the white notes and find your way around.

Your First White Note: C

C is a very commonly used white note. The C's lie directly to the left of each group of two black notes:

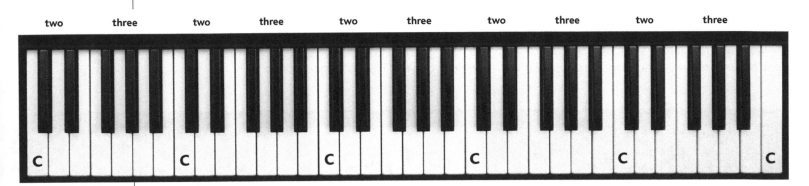

Cut out your C overlays now (included with this book), and place one on each of the C notes.
Note the position of these C's for a moment, then remove the overlays and see if you can locate the C's without them.

The Other Six White Notes

The musical alphabet runs from A to G, then repeats itself over and over again.
In other words, there are only seven different white notes to learn:

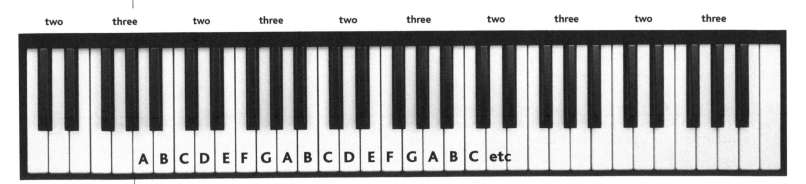

* The exact number of keys varies from model to model.

Your Second White Note: G

The G notes lie here, within each group of three black notes:

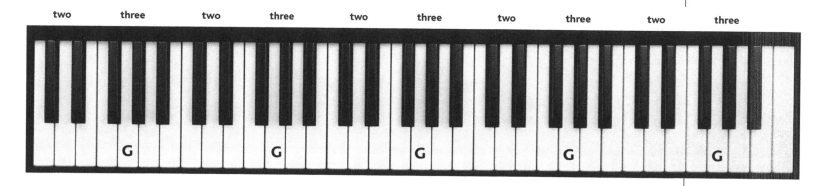

| two | three | two | three | two | three | two | three | two | three |

Cut out your G overlays now, and place them on each of the G notes.
Check out their position for a moment, then remove the overlays and locate all the G notes without them.

Splitting The Keyboard

NO, THIS DOESN'T MEAN chopping it in half! Go to your **auto-accompaniment** control and change the setting from **normal** to **single-finger chords***.

Your keyboard has now been divided electronically into two distinct sections: a MELODY section and an ACCOMPANIMENT section:

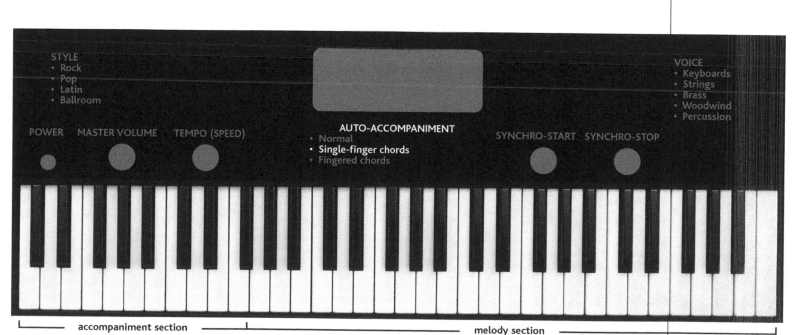

* Your owner's manual will tell you how to select single-finger chords on your particular instrument.

Accompaniment Section

YOUR **ACCOMPANIMENT** SECTION is situated at the bottom end (left hand side) of your keyboard. It will probably have note names (letters) displayed above or below it:

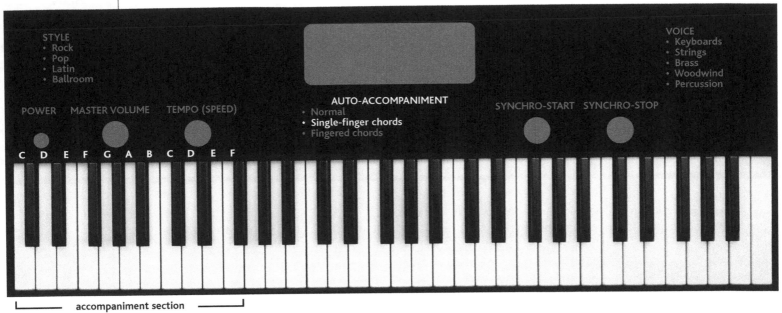

accompaniment section

Accompaniment sections usually run from C to F. Check that you have **single-finger chords** selected, then play any note in your accompaniment section with finger 2 of your left hand.
You are now hearing a **chord** (three notes playing together).

Play a few more single notes at random in your accompaniment section and listen to the chords which your keyboard is playing automatically for you. (NB: You may have to activate your **style** or **rhythm** section to make these single-finger chords work. If so, select any rhythm, say **rock** and press start.)

C and G Chords

Now let's learn two specific chords.
Do you remember how the note C looks, in relation to its two adjacent black keys?

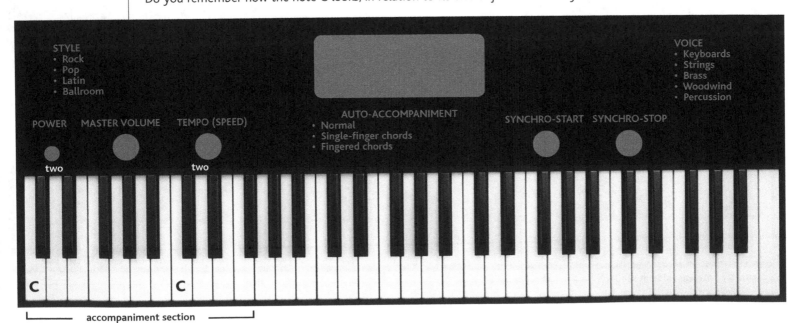

accompaniment section

* accompaniment sections do vary. On some models the accompaniment section range is from C to G; on some models the 'single-finger chord' range is only from C to C. See your owner's manual for more information.

Check that you still have **single-finger chords** set on your keyboard, then play the *higher* of the two C's with your left hand 2nd finger:

C

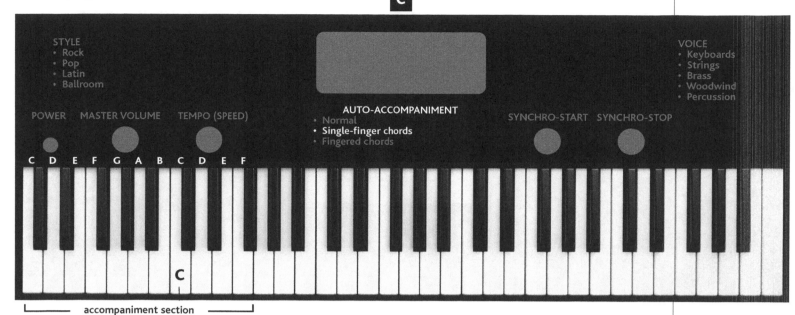

accompaniment section

You are now playing the chord of **C**, which is written in a box, like this: **C**

You can check that you are playing C if your keyboard has letter names printed above the accompaniment section.

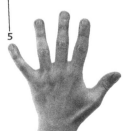

Left Hand

Do you remember how **G** looks, in relation to its three neighbouring black keys?
Play the LOWER of the two G's with your left hand 5th finger:

G

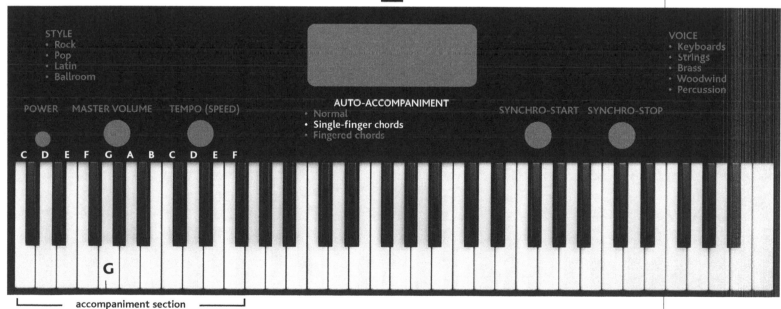

accompaniment section

Check your G against the letters on the keyboard.

You are now playing a chord of G, which is written like this: **G**

Left Hand

Adding Rhythm To Your Chords

IN THE STYLE (RHYTHM) section of your keyboard, select rock pop (or a similar style) and press the SYNCHRO-START button (nothing will happen for the moment).

In your AUTO-ACCOMPANIMENT section, select **single-finger chords**:

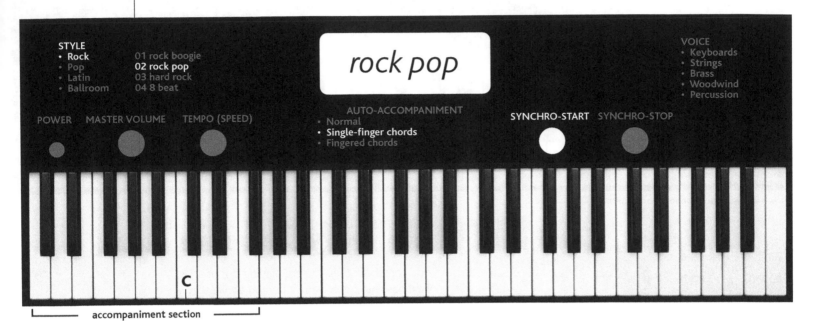

rock pop

STYLE
- **Rock**
- Pop
- Latin
- Ballroom

01 rock boogie
02 rock pop
03 hard rock
04 8 beat

VOICE
- Keyboards
- Strings
- Brass
- Woodwind
- Percussion

POWER   MASTER VOLUME   TEMPO (SPEED)

AUTO-ACCOMPANIMENT
- Normal
- **Single-finger chords**
- Fingered chords

SYNCHRO-START   SYNCHRO-STOP

accompaniment section

Left Hand

Play C (left hand finger 2) and your rhythm section will start up on a chord of **C**.

Now change to G (left hand finger 5) and listen to a chord of **G**.

Alternate between the two chords a few times.
For variation, change the rhythm from **rock pop** to **bossa nova**:

bossa nova

STYLE
- Rock
- Pop
- **Latin**
- Ballroom

01 merengue
02 salsa
03 bossa nova
04 rhumba

VOICE
- Keyboards
- Strings
- Brass
- Woodwind
- Percussion

POWER   MASTER VOLUME   TEMPO (SPEED)

AUTO-ACCOMPANIMENT
- Normal
- **Single-finger chords**
- Fingered chords

SYNCHRO-START   SYNCHRO-STOP

accompaniment section

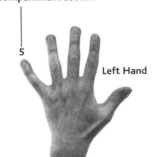

Left Hand

Beats And Bars

WHEN YOU WERE PLAYING, did you feel the natural pulse of the music? Underlying most popular music there are pulses, or **beats**, which have a regularly recurring accent:

beats: **1** 2 3 4 **1** 2 3 4 **1** 2 3 4 (etc.)

When writing this down, vertical lines, called **bar lines**, are placed in front of the first (accented) beat:

beats: | **1** 2 3 4 | **1** 2 3 4 | **1** 2 3 4 | (etc.)

bar lines

As well as denoting the natural accents of the piece, these bar lines divide the music up into **bars**, or **measures**:

bar (measure) 1   bar 2   bar 3

beats: | **1** 2 3 4 | **1** 2 3 4 | **1** 2 3 4 | (etc.)

Playing On The Beat

The following song accompaniment will give you practice in counting beats.

Set up your keyboard as shown at the beginning of the piece, then press **start**.
Listen to the rhythm for a while, then try counting a regular "**1**, **2**, **3**, **4**" to it.
When it sounds right to you, play a chord of C (left hand finger 2), and start following the written music.

After two bars of C, change to a chord of G (left hand finger 5).
Play right through the piece like this, following the music carefully.

White Rose Of Athens – Accompaniment

Style (or rhythm): **8 beat light**
Tempo: **medium (♩=116)**
Single-finger chords: **on**

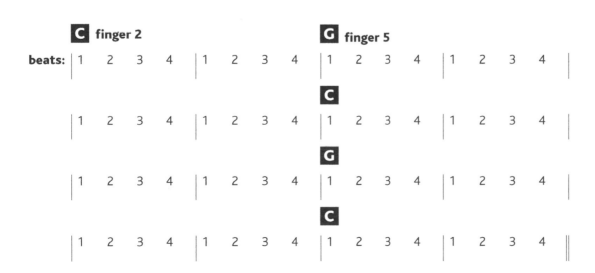

Melody Section

AS YOU LEARNT EARLIER, when you select **single-finger chords** on your keyboard the keyboard splits electronically into two sections:

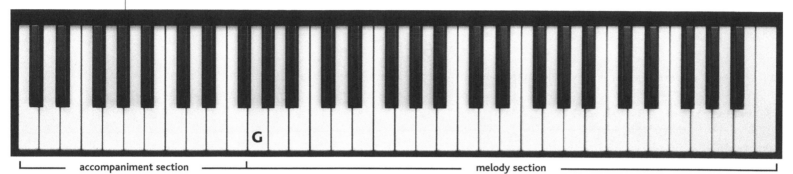

accompaniment section — melody section

The **melody** section usually begins at G, but check with your manual for any differences.

In the **melody** section you play the tune (melody) of the piece, with your right hand. The **voices** (piano, flute, violin etc) apply only to the **melody** section since, when the keyboard is split, the **accompaniment** section has its own fixed sound.

White Rose Of Athens – Melody Only

To play the melody of 'White Rose Of Athens' you need the following five notes, which you play with your right hand:

MIDDLE C (Generally the C closest to the middle of your keyboard)

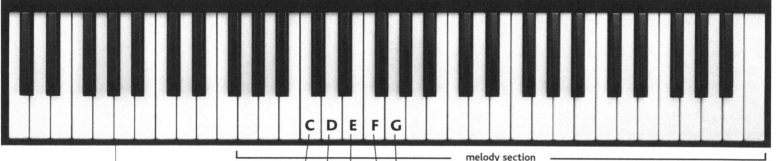

C D E F G

melody section

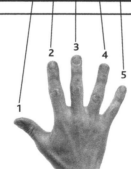

Place the overlays which come with this book over the notes if you need to.

Right Hand

Here are those five melody notes written down:

TREBLE CLEF
(used for right hand notes)

STAVE
(5 horizontal lines)

MIDDLE C   D   E   F   G

The **stave** is a sort of musical 'ladder' upon which the notes are placed. Notes can be placed **on** lines, or in the spaces **between** them. **Middle C** is too low for the stave, so a small temporary line is provided for it below the stave. These little lines (drawn above or below the stave as required) are called **ledger lines**.

White Rose Of Athens – Melody

Voice: **guitar**
Style: **8 beat light**
Tempo: **medium** (♩ = 116)

1   Start with your right thumb (finger 1) on **middle C**, and play the middle C note six times in all, as written.

2   Move up step by step, through D and E, and back to D again. The D note plays eight times in all.

3   Reach up and play G three times with your fifth finger, then move down step by step, through F and E (E plays twice), then back to D (D plays twice).

Follow the song carefully through like this, noting especially when the notes repeat or move by step.

Note Values

IN THE PREVIOUS 'simplified' version of 'White Rose Of Athens' all the notes were the same length and followed the beat exactly. These 'beat' notes, called **quarter notes** or **crotchets**, are written like this:

TIME SIGNATURE
Indicates 4 "quarter notes" (crotchets) per bar

"quarter notes" (crotchets)

beats: 1 2 3 4   1 2 3 4   1 2 3 4   1 2 3 4

Of course tunes do not slavishly follow the beat like this as a rule.
Rather they employ a mixture of **long** and **short** notes:

Note Values

♩ or ♩	**quarter note (crotchet)**	1 beat
♩ or ♩	**half note (minim)**	hold for 2 beats
♩. or ♩.	**dotted half note (dotted minim)**	hold for 3 beats
o	**whole note (semibreve)**	hold for 4 beats

In the final (correct) version of 'White Rose Of Athens' (facing page), some of the melody notes fall on the beat, others must be held longer:

LONG NOTE   **LONG NOTE**   **TIE** (hold this note for 8 beats in all)

bar 1   bar 2   bar 3   bar 4

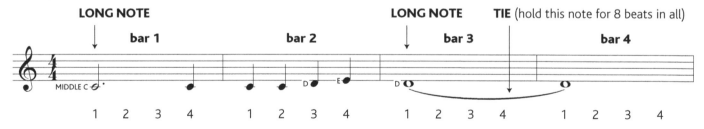

1 2 3 4   1 2 3 4   1 2 3 4   1 2 3 4

Ties

Any note can be made to last longer by means of a **tie**:

TIE   **TIE**

total length of note = 6 beats   total length of last note = 2 beats

Work through the whole of 'White Rose Of Athens' now, right hand only, counting the beats and playing and holding down the notes correctly, as indicated by the music. When you have mastered the right hand try adding the left hand chords.

White Rose Of Athens

Original Words & Music by Manos Hadjidakis & Hans Bradtke | English Words by Norman Newell | Additional Words by Archie Bleyer

Voice: **mandolin (or folk guitar)**
Style: **(Rhythm) 8 beat light**
Tempo: **medium (♩ = 116)**

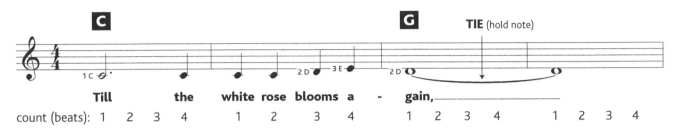

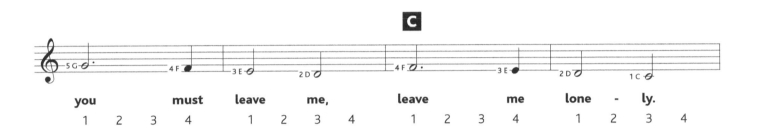

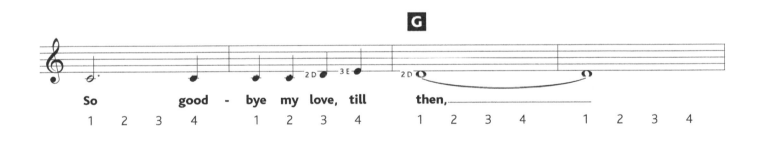

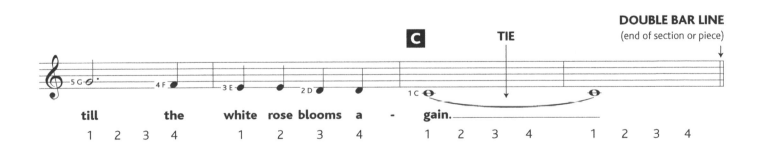

Fingered Chords

UP TO NOW you have been using a 'single-finger' chord system in your left hand. You can stay with single-finger chords for the rest of this course and beyond, if you wish, but if you want to develop your musical potential to the full you should think of changing to real chords – in other words, **fingered chords**, now:

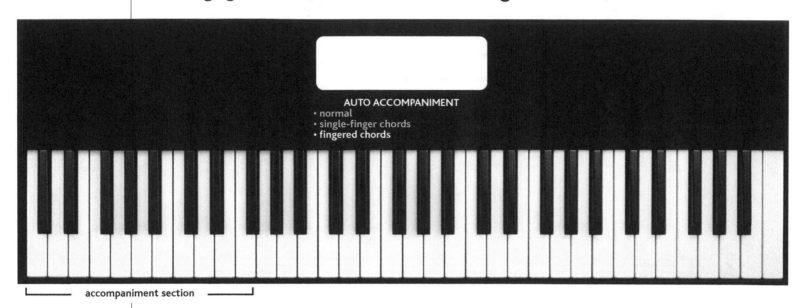

AUTO ACCOMPANIMENT
• normal
• single-finger chords
• **fingered chords**

accompaniment section

Here are your first two fingered chords:

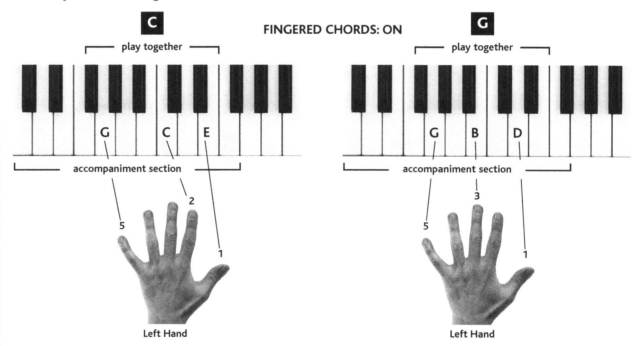

FINGERED CHORDS: ON

Play the two chords separately at first, to get the feel of them, then try moving from one to the other. Since the bottom note **G** is common to both chords, it is good practice to hold it down during the changes.

Fingered Chord Exercise 1

Style (Rhythm): **Rock**
Tempo: **Medium (♩ = 112)**
Fingered chords: **On**

Repeat sign
go back to the opposite facing sign and repeat

New Chord: F

Single-finger chord method:
SINGLE-FINGER CHORDS ON

Fingered chord method:
FINGERED CHORDS ON

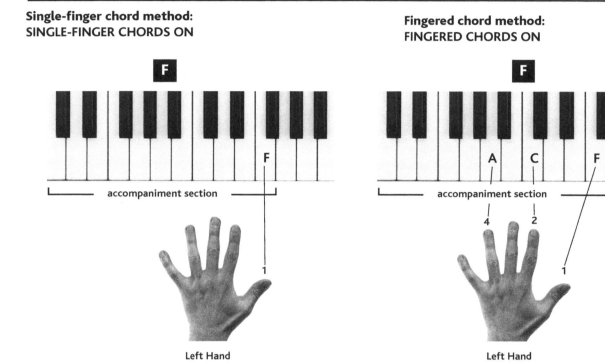

Fingered Chord Exercise 2

Fingered chords: **On**
Rhythm: **Rock**
Tempo: **Medium**

Hold down middle note (**C**) throughout (optional)

Fingered Chord Exercise 3

Fingered chords: **On**
Rhythm: **Rock**
Tempo: **Medium**

Playing Legato

LEGATO is an Italian word, meaning *smooth, joined-up*. As you play through the melodies of the next two songs, walk very precisely from finger to finger, releasing the old finger exactly as the new finger goes down. There should be no breaks in sound between the notes, nor ugly overlaps. This joined-up style of playing is called legato. **You always play legato, unless the music is marked otherwise.**

Bye Bye Love

Words & Music by Felice & Boudleaux Bryant

The Everly Brothers

Voice: **Vibraphone**
Style: **Swing**
Tempo: **Fairly fast** (♩=132)

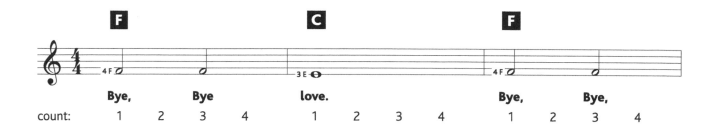

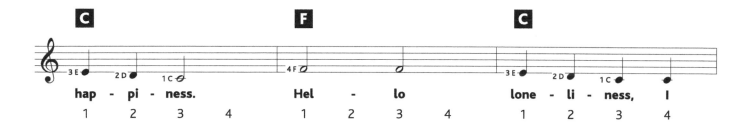

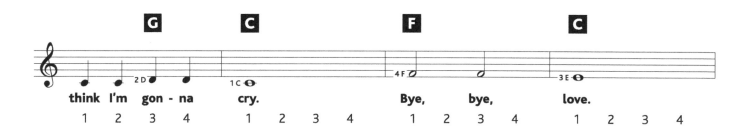

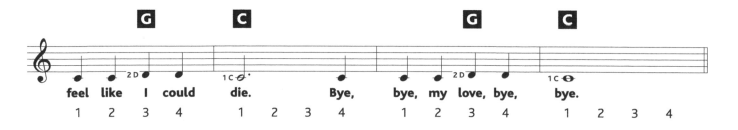

Creedence Clearwater Revival

Bad Moon Rising

Words & Music by John C. Fogerty

Voice: **Distorted Guitar**
Style: **8 Beat Pop**
Tempo: **Medium** (♩=150)

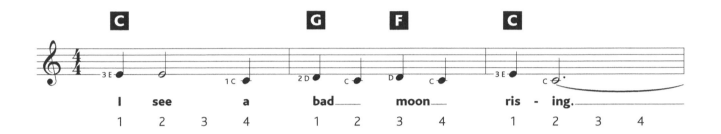

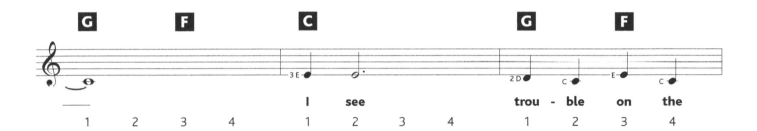

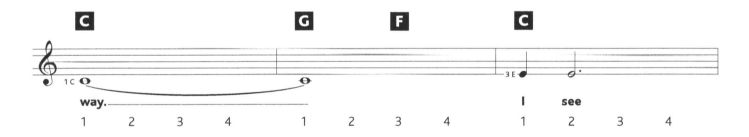

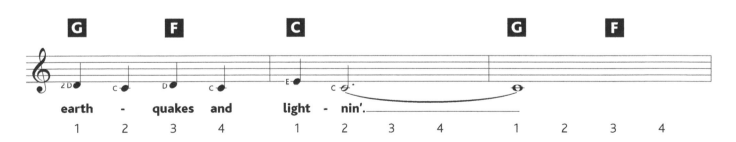

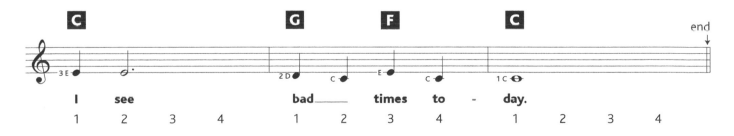

Pick-Up Notes

SONGS DO NOT ALWAYS begin on beat 1. In your next song, 'One More Night' by Phil Collins, the melody actually begins on beat 2:

One More Night (excerpt)

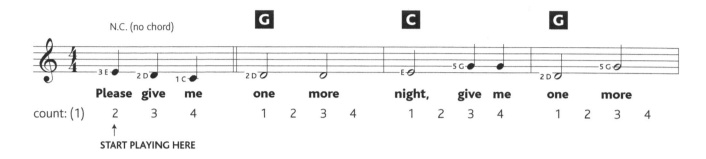

The three preliminary notes at the beginning of 'One More Night' are called pick-up notes.

Beats missing from the pick-up bar appear (usually) in the last bar of the song:

One More Night (excerpt)

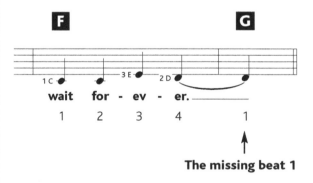

Arranging things in this way means that you can go around the song again if you wish, keeping the beats intact.

NOTE: It is usual to play *no chord* (written N.C.) during pick-up notes.

Synchro (Synchro-Start)

IT IS WITH SONGS beginning with pick-up notes that the SYNCHRO-START feature becomes useful.

When you activate your **synchro** button your rhythm section does not begin until you play the first left hand chord. This makes a neat beginning to the song.

One More Night

Words & Music by Phil Collins

Phil Collins

Voice: **alto saxophone**
Style: **16 beat ballad**
Tempo: **medium (♩=92)**
Synchro-start: **on**

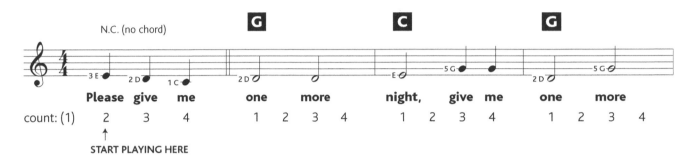

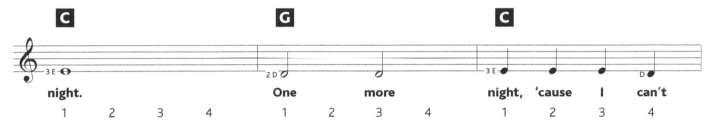

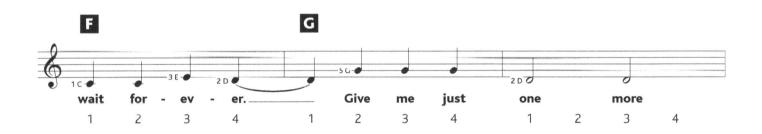

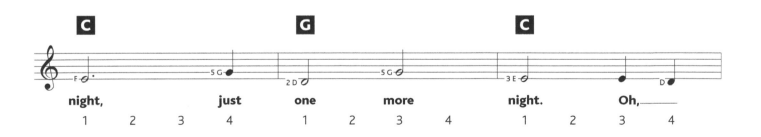

Three New Notes: A, B, C

FOR RIGHT HAND

Fingering The New Notes

NOW THAT YOU are moving beyond the original playing range of your five fingers, new fingering techniques will have to be adopted if the music is to remain legato.

Rio Grande (excerpt)

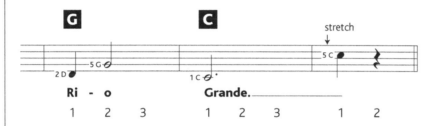

Don't jump here – stretch out for the high C.

Mr Tambourine Man (excerpt)

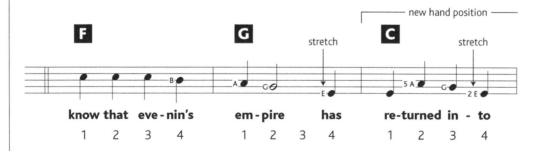

In **bar 3**, stretch out a little to play the E.

In **bar 4**, squeeze together a little to pick up the new hand position, then stretch out to play E and C.

Remember: as soon as you have completed any stretching movements in a song, let your hand return to its normal, relaxed five finger playing position (see page 5).

Rests

SILENCES ARE OFTEN called for in music. In order to indicate these, symbols called **rests** are used. Each note value has its own rest:

TIME NOTE		REST SILENCE	LASTING
♩	quarter note (crotchet)	𝄽	1 beat
♩	half note (minim)	▬	2 beats
♩.	dotted half note (dotted minim)	▬·	3 beats
o	whole note (semibreve)	▬	4 beats, or one whole bar regardless of time signature

Rests are used mainly for musical or dramatic reasons. However, they are also useful for moving your hand from one part of the keyboard to another:

Rio Grande (excerpt)

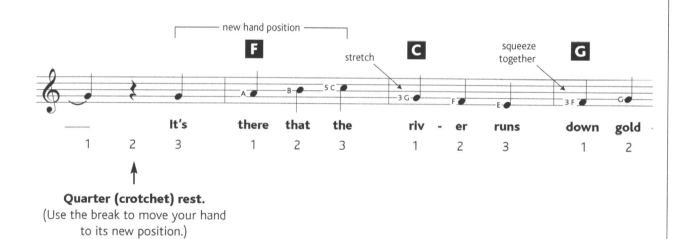

Quarter (crotchet) rest.
(Use the break to move your hand
to its new position.)

Waltz Time

SO FAR ALL OUR SONGS have been in four-four time (4/4).

However, many popular songs have **three** beats to the bar, rather than four. Songs in 3/4 time (3 quarter notes per bar) are called **Waltzes**. Our next song, 'Rio Grande', is a waltz.

Rio Grande

Traditional

Voice: **harmonica**
Style: **country waltz**
Tempo: **medium** (♩ = 100)
Synchro-start: **on**

VERSES*

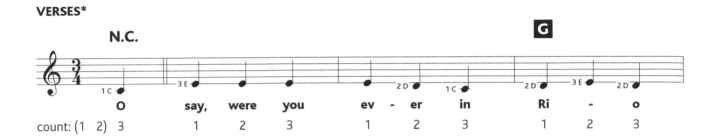

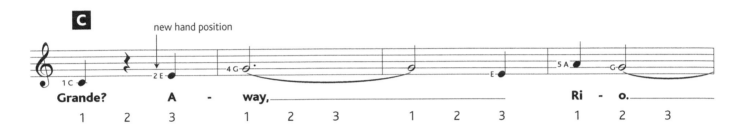

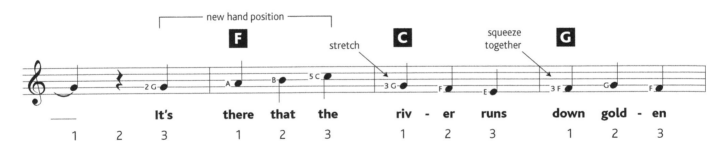

CHORUS**

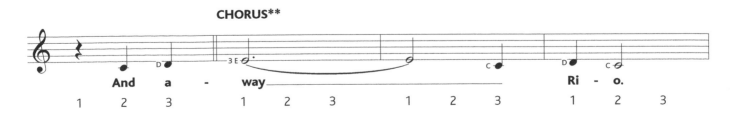

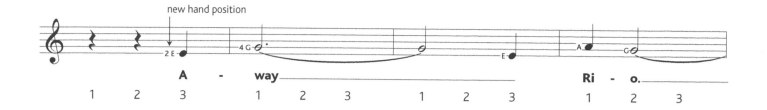

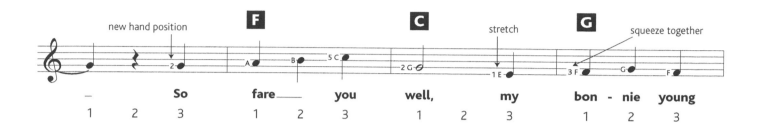

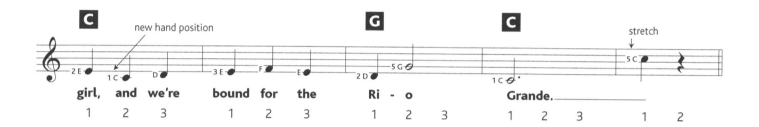

Continuing verses:

Verse 2
Oh, New York City is no place for me, away, Rio
I'll pack my bags and then I'll go out to sea
And we're bound for the Rio Grande
And away, Rio (etc.)

Verse 3
The anchor's aweigh and the sails they are set, away, Rio
The girls we are leaving we'll never forget
And we're bound for the Rio Grande
And away, Rio (etc.)

Verse 4
So pack up your sea bag and get underway, away, Rio
Perhaps we'll return again another day
And we're bound for the Rio Grande
And away, Rio (etc.)

Verse 5
A jolly good mate and a jolly good crew, away, Rio
A jolly good ship and a good skipper too
And we're bound for the Rio Grande
And away, Rio (etc.)

Verse 6
Now you lovely ladies, we would let you know, away, Rio
That the time has come, and we're about to go
And we're bound for the Rio Grande
And away, Rio (etc.)

Verse 7
Sing goodbye to Sally, and goodbye to Sue, away, Rio
And to all you listening, it's goodbye too
And we're bound for the Rio Grande
And away, Rio (etc.)

Bob Dylan

Blowin' In The Wind

Words & Music by Bob Dylan

Voice: **oboe**
Style: **8 beat ballad**
Tempo: **medium** (♩ = 104)

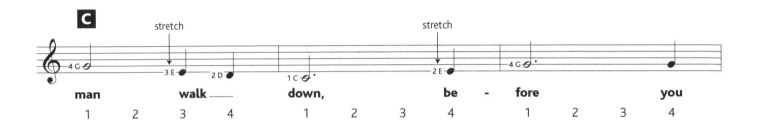

	How		ma -	ny	roads		must	a
count:	1	2	3	4	1	2	3	4

man		walk		down,			be -	fore			you
1	2	3	4	1	2	3	4	1	2	3	4

call		him	a	man?						Yes,	'n'
1	2	3	4	1	2	3	4	1	2	3	4

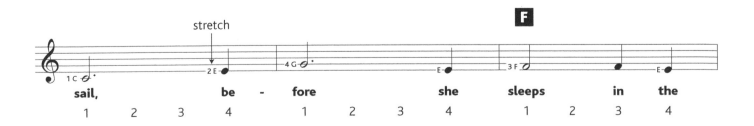

how		ma -	ny	seas		must	a	white		dove	
1	2	3	4	1	2	3	4	1	2	3	4

sail,			be -	fore			she	sleeps	in	the	
1	2	3	4	1	2	3	4	1	2	3	4

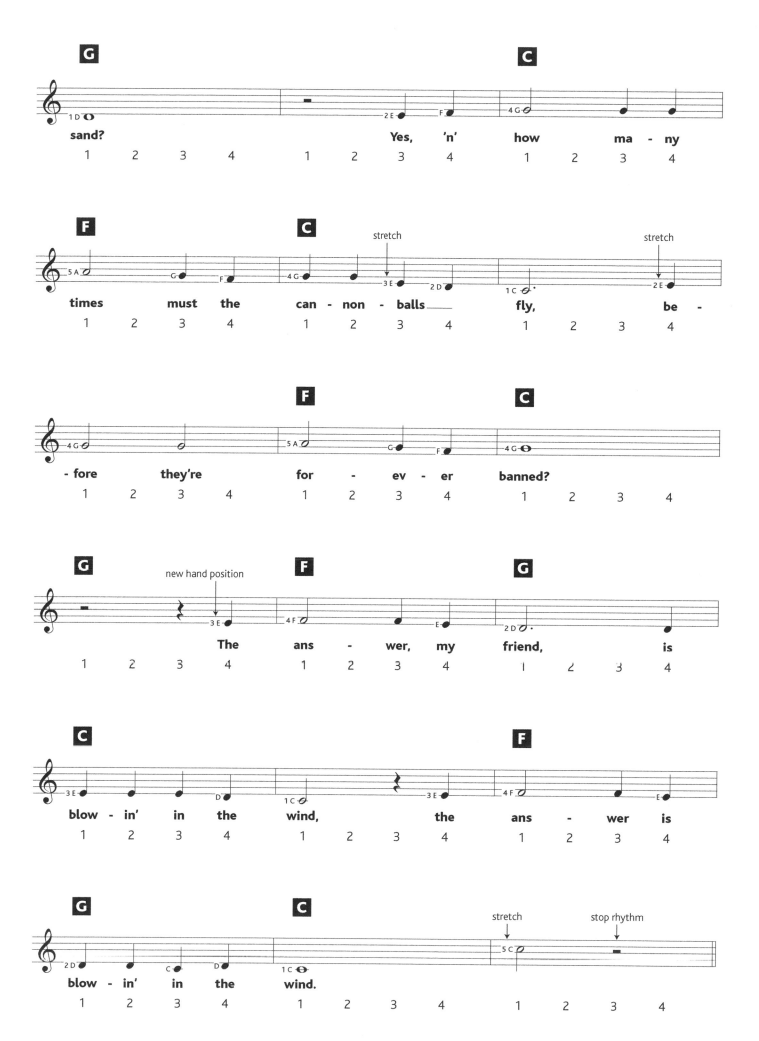

Mr. Tambourine Man

Words & Music by Bob Dylan

Bob Dylan

Voice: **12 string guitar**
Style: **8 beat light**
Tempo: **medium (♩ = 116)**
Synchro-start: **on**

VERSE

Tho' I know that eve - nin's em - pire has re-turned in - to

count: (1 2) 3 4 1 2 3 4 1 2 3 4 1 2 3 4

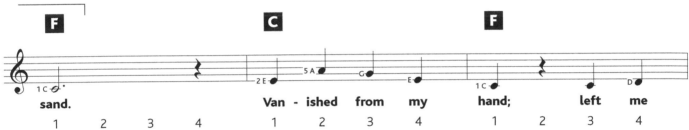

sand. Van - ished from my hand; left me

1 2 3 4 1 2 3 4 1 2 3 4

blind - ly here to stand, but still not sleep - in'.

1 2 3 4 1 2 3 4 1 2 3 4

My wear - i - ness a - ma - zes me, I'm

1 2 3 4 1 2 3 4 1 2 3 4

brand - ed on my feet; I have no - one to

1 2 3 4 1 2 3 4 1 2 3 4

31

New Right Hand Notes: D, E, F, G

Pete Seeger

Where Have All The Flowers Gone?

Words & Music by Pete Seeger

Voice: **flute**
Style: **8 beat ballad**
Tempo: **medium** (♩ = 100)

Eighth Notes (Quavers)

THE EIGHTH NOTE, or **quaver**, is a new note value:

Eighth notes move twice as fast as quarter notes:

In other words, if a quarter note is worth one beat, an eighth note is worth half a beat. If you say the word 'and' in between the beat numbers you will get the feel of the eighth note:

| count: | 1 | 2 | 3 | 4 | | 1 | and | 2 | and | 3 | and | 4 | and |

Keep the basic beats very regular here, then fit the quaver notes *exactly* in between them.

Like all the other note values, the eighth note has its own rest:

Eighth (quaver) rest   equivalent to   lasting

❼   ♪   ¹/₂ beat

Count eighth rests in exactly the same way that you would count eighth notes:

Yellow (excerpt)

	Look at the stars	**look how they shine**	**for**	**you,**
	I came a-long,	I wrote a song	for	you,
count:	1 and 2 and 3 4	1 and 2 and 3 4		2 3 4

Yellow

Words & Music by Guy Berryman, Jon Buckland, Will Champion & Chris Martin

Coldplay

Voice: **piano**
Style: **8 beat light**
Tempo: **slow** (♩ = 86)

Imagine

Words & Music by John Lennon

John Lennon

Voice: **piano**
Style: **slow ballad**
Tempo: **slow** (♩ = 80)

I - ma - gine there's no   hea - ven,   it's ea - sy if   you

count: 1 and 2 and 3   4   1   2   3   4   1 and 2 and 3   4

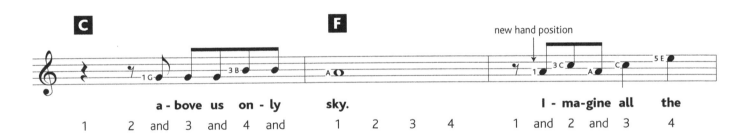

try.   **No hell** be - low us,

1   2   3   4   1   2 and 3   4   1   2   3   4

new hand position

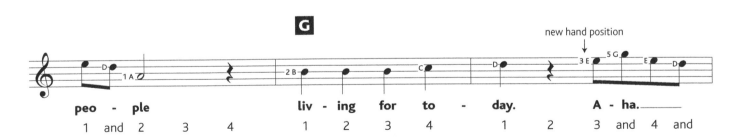

a - bove us on - ly   sky.   **I** - ma - gine all   the

1   2 and 3 and 4 and   1   2   3   4   1 and 2 and 3   4

new hand position

peo - ple   liv - ing for to - day.   A - ha.

1 and 2   3   4   1   2   3   4   1   2   3 and 4 and

new hand position

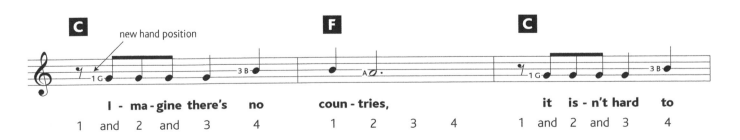

I - ma - gine there's   no   coun - tries,   it   is - n't hard   to

1 and 2 and 3   4   1   2   3   4   1 and 2 and 3   4

Legato And Staccato

AS YOU KNOW, **legato** means joined up or connected. When you play legato you move smoothly from finger to finger, leaving no gaps between notes. Notes which are to be played legato are often indicated on the music by a curved line called a **slur** or **phrase mark**:

Do Wah Diddy Diddy (excerpt)

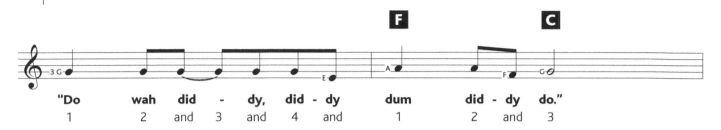

"Do	wah	did	-	dy,	did	-	dy	dum	did	-	dy	do."
1	2	and		3	and		4	and	1	2	and	3

When there are no slurs or other markings to the contrary, play legato.

When a single note amongst a group of staccato notes is to be played legato, it is sometimes marked like this, and called **tenuto**:

Seasons In The Sun (excerpt)

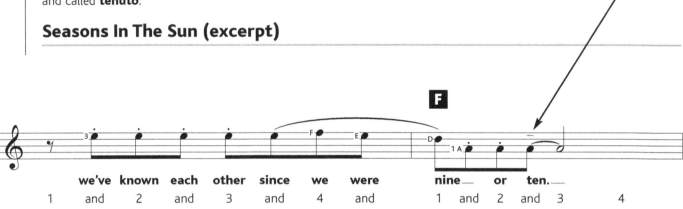

	we've	known	each	other	since	we	were		nine—	or	ten.—	
1	and	2	and	3	and	4	and	1	and	2	and 3	4

The opposite of legato is **staccato**, which means 'cut short'.

To play staccato, release the note as soon as it has been played, using a sort of 'pecking' movement of the hand. Notes which are to be played staccato are indicated on the music by dots above or below the note:

Do Wah Diddy Diddy (excerpt)

	1. There	she was,	just a
	we're	to - ge - ther	near - ly
count:	1	2 and 3	4 and

Do Wah Diddy Diddy

Words & Music by Jeff Barry & Ellie Greenwich

Manfred Mann

Voice: **trumpet**
Style: **8-beat up-tempo**
Tempo: **medium (♩ = 120)**
Synchro-start: **on**

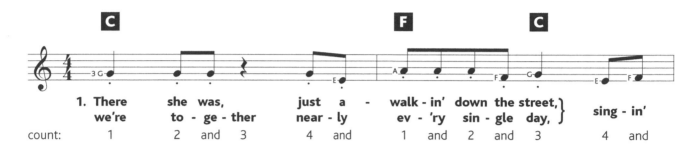

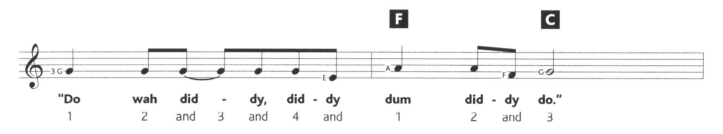

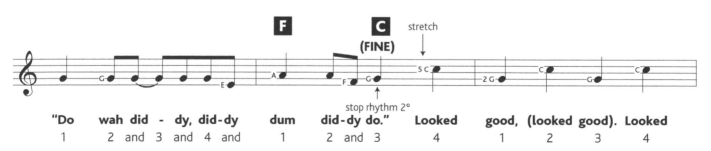

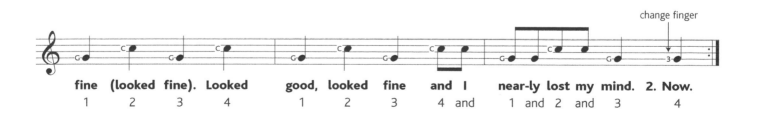

Westlife

Seasons In The Sun

Words by Rod McKuen | Music by Jacques Brel

Voice: **accordion**
Style: **slow rock**
Tempo: **medium (♩ = 88)**

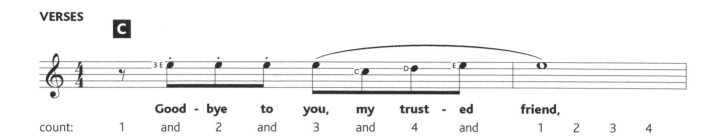

VERSES

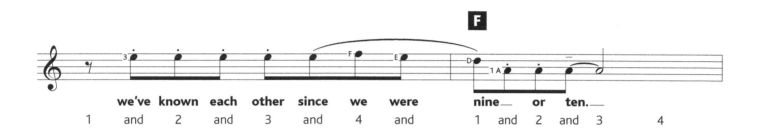

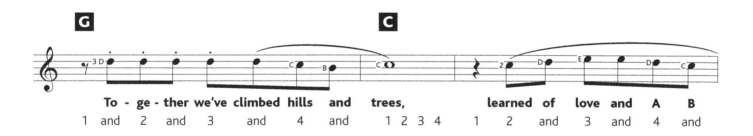

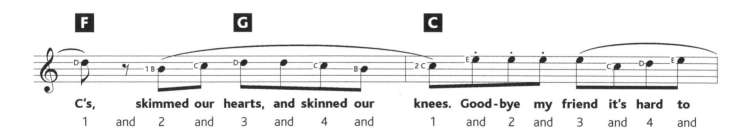

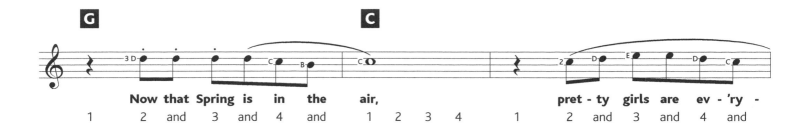

Now that Spring is in the air,
1 2 and 3 and 4 and 1 2 3 4

pret - ty girls are ev - 'ry -
1 2 and 3 and 4 and

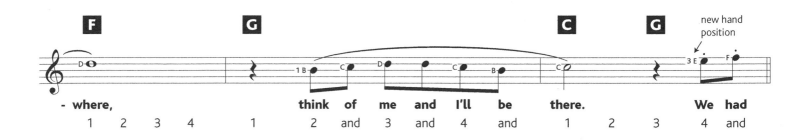

- where,
1 2 3 4 1

think of me and I'll be there.
2 and 3 and 4 and 1 2 3 4 and

We had

new hand position

CHORUS

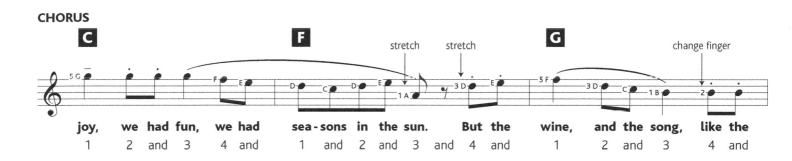

joy, we had fun, we had
1 2 and 3 4 and

sea - sons in the sun.
1 and 2 and 3 and 4 and

But the

stretch   stretch

wine, and the song, like the
1 2 and 3 4 and

change finger

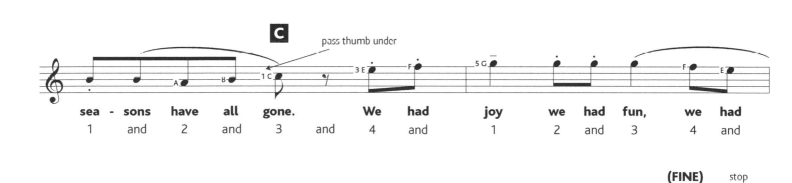

sea - sons have all gone.
1 and 2 and 3 and 4 and

We had
1

joy we had fun, we had
2 and 3 4 and

pass thumb under

(FINE)   stop

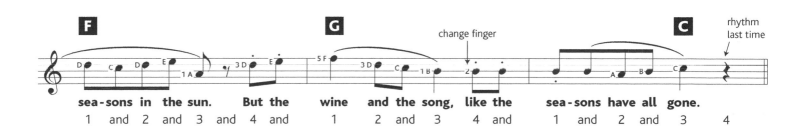

sea - sons in the sun.
1 and 2 and 3 and 4 and

But the
1

wine and the song, like the
2 and 3 4 and

change finger

sea - sons have all gone.
1 and 2 and 3 4

rhythm last time

Seventh Chords

The three chords you have learnt so far: **C**, **G** and **F**, are all **major** chords. **Seventh** chords are *variations* of these chords. When using the single-finger chord method there are various ways of forming sevenths. Your owner's manual will tell you exactly how to form sevenths on your particular instrument, but the first two diagrams below show two possibilities:

Chord Of G7

Single-finger chord method

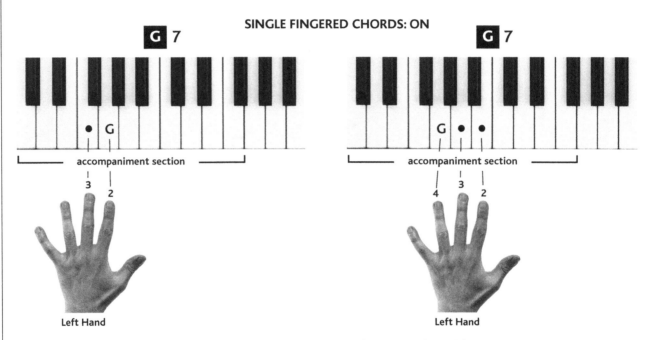

SINGLE FINGERED CHORDS: ON

Play G, together with any white note to its LEFT.

Play G, together with any two notes to its RIGHT.

Fingered chord method

FINGERED CHORDS: ON

Chord Of D7

Single-finger chord method

SINGLE FINGERED CHORDS: ON

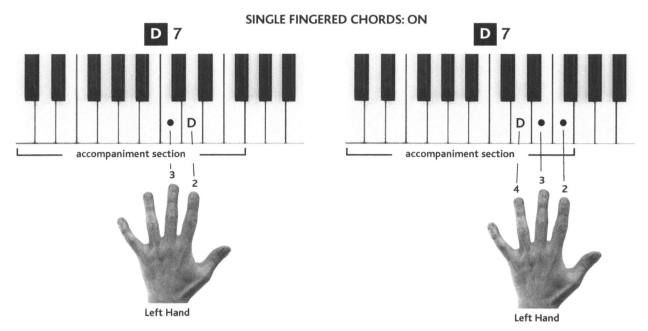

Left Hand

Left Hand

Play D, together with any white note to its LEFT.

Play D, together with any two notes to its RIGHT.

Fingered chord method

FINGERED CHORDS: ON

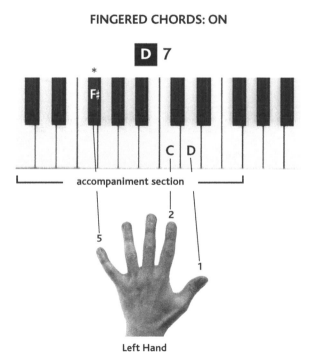

Left Hand

* This symbol ♯ is called a **sharp**. It will be explained properly in Book 2, but for now simply play the black note indicated.

D.S. Al Coda And D.C. Al Coda

WE USE THESE instructions (also known as form notation) to simplify and shorten pieces of music with many repeats. Here are the main terms, and what they mean. Look out for them in the next two pieces.

DAL SEGNO (D.S.) means repeat from the sign 𝄋
FINE is the end of the piece
DAL SEGNO AL FINE (D.S. al FINE) means go back to the sign 𝄋 and play through the piece again until you reach the word FINE. This is where the piece ends.
DA CAPO means the beginning
DA CAPO (D.C.) means 'repeat from the beginning'
DA CAPO AL FINE (D.C. al FINE) means go back to the beginning of the piece and play through again until you reach the word FINE. This is where the piece ends.

Stephen Gately

Any Dream Will Do

Music by Andrew Lloyd Webber | Lyrics by Tim Rice

Voice: **string ensemble**
Style: **swing**
Tempo: **medium (♩ = 125)**
Synchro-start: **on**

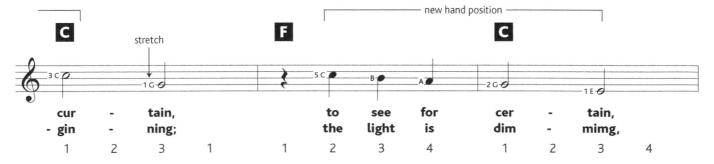

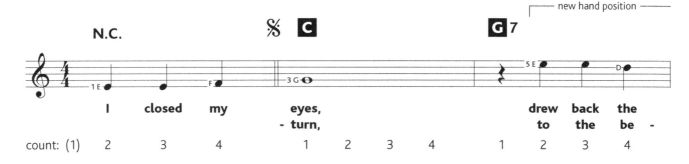

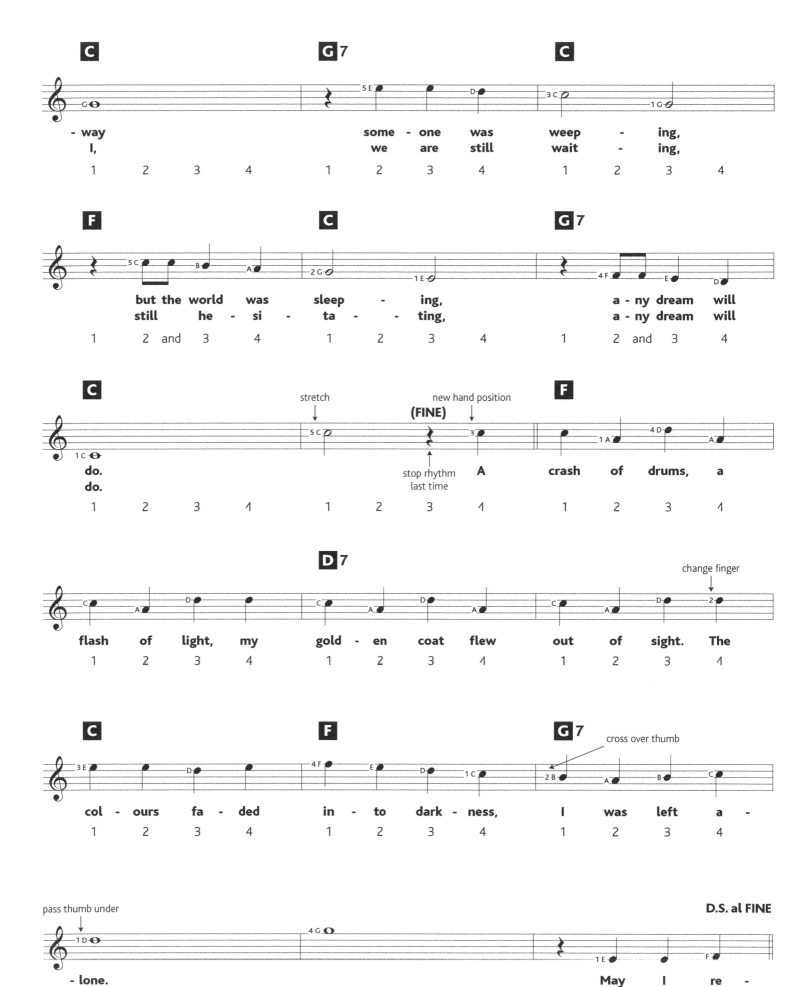

Can You Feel The Love Tonight

(from Walt Disney Pictures' "The Lion King")   Music by Elton John | Words by Tim Rice

Elton John

Voice: **piano**
Style: **16 beat ballad**
Tempo: **slow (♩ = 72)**

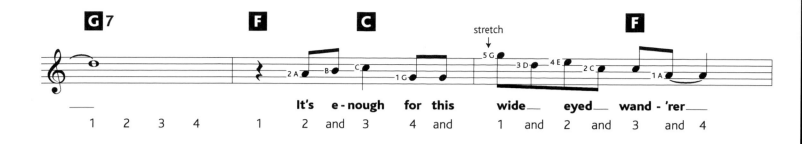

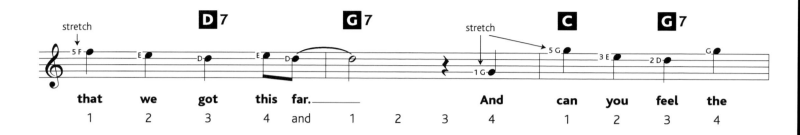

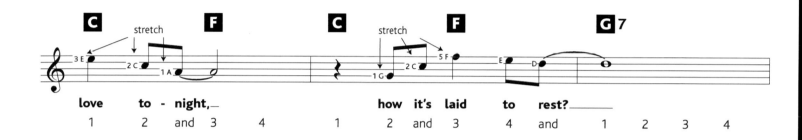

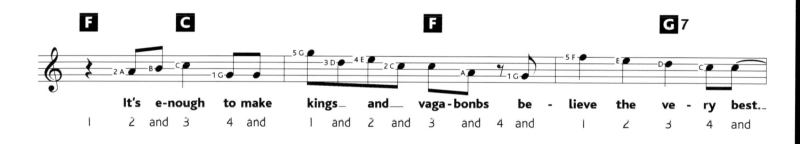

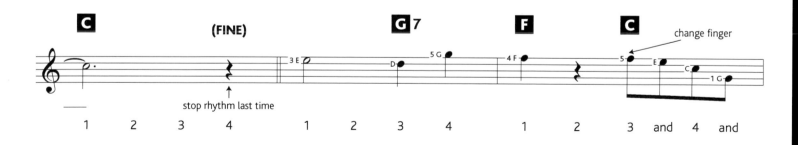

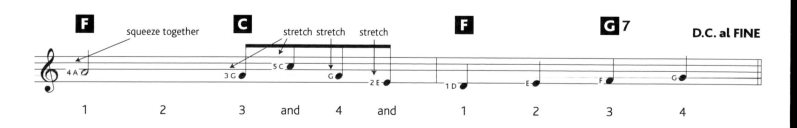

Let It Be

Words & Music by John Lennon & Paul McCartney

Paul McCartney

Voice: **folk guitar**
Style: **light pop**
Tempo: **slow** (♩ = 66)
Synchro-start: **on**

* Use your volume pedal, if you have one. If not, ease back your Master Volume control bit by bit with your left hand in between playing chords.

Congratulations

... on completing Book 1 of The Complete Keyboard Player!

In Book 2 you will...

- Learn about sharps and flats ■ Move to a new stage in note reading ■ Increase the range of your melody playing
- Learn new left hand chords, including minor chords ■ Add to your repertoire of great popular songs!